The NatureTrail Book of WILD FLOWERS

Sue Tarsky

Identifying Wild Flowers
with this Book

This book is about common European wild flowers you can
find. It tells you how and where they live, and how they grow.
When you find a wild flower, and you want to know its name,
or more about it, use this book as follows:

1 Turn to the pages which deal
with the **kind of place** where
you found the flower. For
example, pages 24–25 tell you
about flowers in towns. If
you can't see it there . . .

2 Turn to the back of the book
(pages 28–31) and look it up
in the section called **Other
Common Flowers to Spot**
where you may be able to
find a picture of it.

If you still can't find it, look on other pages in the book,
such as page 14, where there is a Flower Calendar, or page 7
in the section How to Recognize Flowers. Always make
careful notes about flowers you find, and try to identify
them later.

The name Usborne and the device are
Trade Marks of Usborne Publishing Ltd.

First published in 1976 by
Usborne Publishing Ltd,
20 Garrick Street,
London WC2

Text and Artwork © 1976 by
Usborne Publishing Ltd.

ISBN ON BACK COVER?

Foxglove

Marsh Marigold

**Wood
Anemone**

Written by
Sue Tarsky

Series Editor
Sue Jacquemier

Consultant Editors
Sally Heathcote, B.Sc.
Jean Mellanby

Designed by
Nick Eddison

Illustrated by
David Ashby, David Baxter,
Hilary Burn, Liz Butler,
Patrick Cox, Victoria Gordon,
Colin King, Deborah King,
David Nash, Gwen Simpson,
George Thompson, Joan Thompson
Joyce Tuhill, Phil Weare.

Printed in Belgium

Dog Rose

The NatureTrail Book of
WILD FLOWERS

This book tells you where to look for common European wild flowers and how best to study them. It shows you some special things to notice about them, how they grow, and how to collect information and note down what you see. If you want to identify a wild flower, follow the instructions on page 1.

If you have enjoyed this book, you may want to look at some field guides. There is a list on page 32, along with a list of wild flower clubs you can join.

Contents

Herb Robert

Bluebell

Speedwell

Looking for Wild Flowers

When you go looking for wild flowers, take a notebook and two pencils with you for making quick sketches. Write down everything about a flower as soon as you see it. A magnifying glass is useful for looking at the small parts, and a tape measure for finding its height. Don't dig up flowers, and only pick them if you are sure they are common, and there are lots of the same kind growing together. Take sheets of newspaper to press the flowers. Use an outdoor thermometer to note the air temperature.

What You Need

Pencil
Notebook
Magnifying glass
Book with newspaper
Thermometer
Tape measure

July 12th 1975
Trent meadows. 20°C

flowers are yellow

flower heads are 20mm across

flowers are flat on top

flowers look like daisy

plant has hairs

leaves are oval and pointed at ends

leaves have wavy edges

plant is 40cm high

Magnifying glass

Petal
Stamens
Sepal
Stigma
Ovary

This is what the inside of a Buttercup looks like. Other flowers may look different. Try to draw what you see inside the flower you have found.

4

The three flowers shown on the right are very rare indeed. If you think you may have found a rare wild flower, do not pick it. If you do, it will die and be even more rare. Instead, draw the flower and show your drawing to an adult who knows about rare flowers.

If it is rare, you can report it to a conservation or nature club in your area. An expert may be able to gather some seeds when they fall from the flower and plant them carefully so that they will grow.

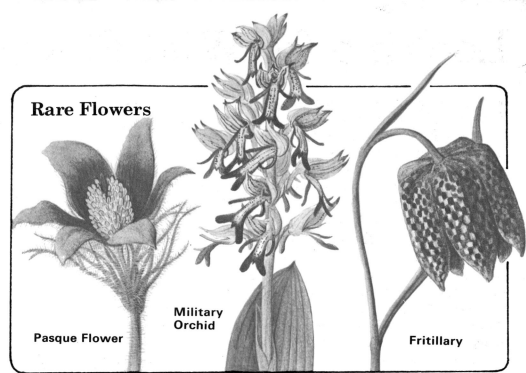

Rare Flowers

Pasque Flower

Military Orchid

Fritillary

50 paces

Symbols for your map

- ✩ FLOWERS
- 🍄 WOODS
- ∼ STREAM
- ⼿ GRASSLAND
- ⋀ HILLS
- ⼿ MARSHES, WATER
- ⎓ BRIDGE
- ⌂⌂ HOUSES

How to Make a Flower Map

The easiest way to make a map is to draw it as you walk along a route you know well. Draw lines for the road or path and make it turn in the same way that you do. Put in symbols for bridges, buildings and other special places. Wherever you find a wild flower, mark the place on your map with a star.

Draw the symbols and write what they stand for on the bottom of your map so that everyone can understand them. If you like, you can use a scale to show distance so that anyone can follow your map. You can choose any scale you want. This map shows that 2 cm. is equal to 50 paces.

How Plants Live

The Rosebay Willowherb and the Field Buttercup have flowers with petals and sepals, and also leaves, stems and roots. Most other plants have the same parts, but they are often different shapes and sizes.

Each part of the plant does at least one special thing that helps the plant to live. The leaves make food for the plant. During the day, they take in carbon dioxide, a gas in the air, and together with the green colouring of the leaves, water and sunlight, make food. The leaves take in gases and give out gases and water through holes that are so small that you cannot see them, even with a magnifying glass.

The flower is a very important part of the plant. It is here that the seeds grow.

The petals may be brightly coloured or scented to attract insects. Some flowers need insects to carry pollen to other flowers for pollination (see page 72), so the brighter the colours, the more insects the flower will attract.

The sepals protect the flower when it is in bud. When the flower opens, they lie underneath the petals. All the sepals together are called the calyx.

The leaves make food and "breathe" for the plant. They also get rid of any water that the plant does not need. Because leaves need light to make food, the whole plant grows towards light. Some plants close their leaves at night.

The stem carries water from the roots to the leaves, and carries food made in the leaves to the rest of the plant. It also holds the leaves up to the light.

Rosebay Willowherb

Field Buttercup

The roots hold the plant firmly in the ground, and take up water from the soil that the plant needs.

How to Recognize Flowers

Colour

The easiest thing to notice first about a flower is its colour. A few examples are shown below. But you should also look at the shape of its petals, sepals and leaves.

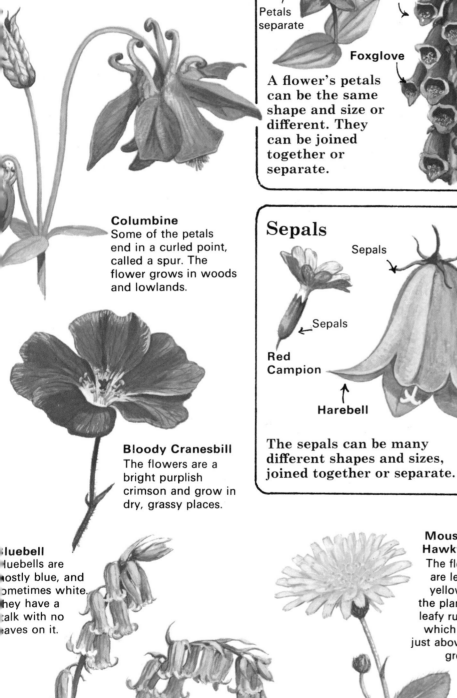

Columbine
Some of the petals end in a curled point, called a spur. The flower grows in woods and lowlands.

Bloody Cranesbill
The flowers are a bright purplish crimson and grow in dry, grassy places.

Bluebell
Bluebells are mostly blue, and sometimes white. They have a stalk with no leaves on it.

Mouse-ear Hawkweed
The flowers are lemon-yellow and the plant has leafy runners which grow just above the ground.

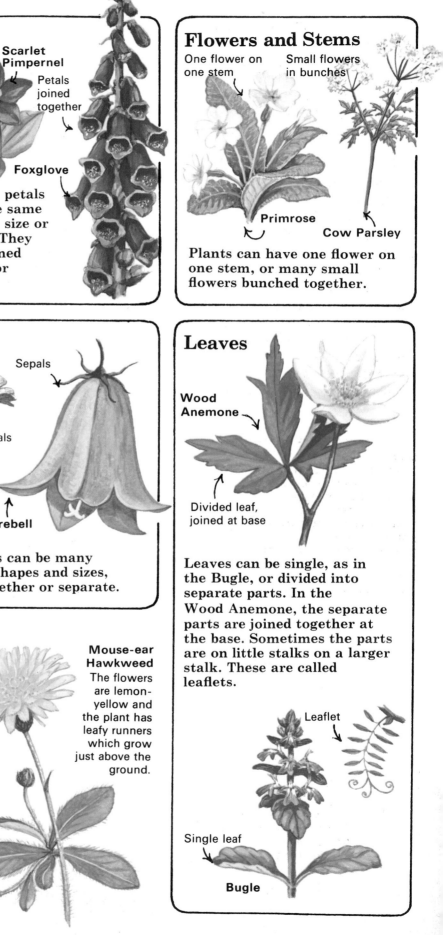

Petals

Scarlet Pimpernel

Petals joined together

Petals separate

Foxglove

A flower's petals can be the same shape and size or different. They can be joined together or separate.

Flowers and Stems

One flower on one stem

Small flowers in bunches

Primrose

Cow Parsley

Plants can have one flower on one stem, or many small flowers bunched together.

Sepals

Sepals

Sepals

Red Campion

Harebell

The sepals can be many different shapes and sizes, joined together or separate.

Leaves

Wood Anemone

Divided leaf, joined at base

Leaves can be single, as in the Bugle, or divided into separate parts. In the Wood Anemone, the separate parts are joined together at the base. Sometimes the parts are on little stalks on a larger stalk. These are called leaflets.

Leaflet

Single leaf

Bugle

How Flowers Grow

Almost every plant has a male part, called the stamen, and a female part, called the pistil. The Common Poppy has a group of stamens which grow around the pistil in the centre of the flower (see no. 3).

This page tells you how the stamens and the pistil in a Poppy together make seeds, which will later leave the plant and grow to form new plants. Not all plants make seeds in this way, but many do.

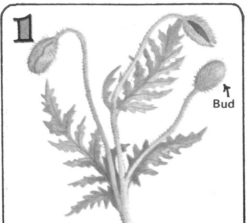

1

Bud

In the spring the new plant grows from a seed buried in the ground. There may be several flowers on one plant.

2

The sepals protect the flower when it is in bud. As the flower grows, the sepals begin to open.

6

As bees fly from flower to flower, the pollen from one poppy may rub off their bodies and onto the stigma of another poppy. This is called pollination.

At the top of the pistil is the **stigma**. At the bottom is an **ovary**, holding **ovules**.

Stigma }
} Pistil
Ovary }

When the pollen grains have landed on top of the stigma, very thin tubes begin to grow down towards the ovary.

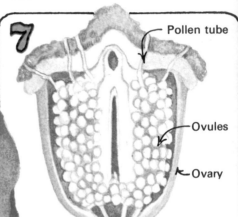

7

Pollen tube

Ovules

Ovary

The tubes eventually reach the ovules in the ovary. The contents of each pollen grain empty into an ovule. This is called fertilization.

11

Holes

The fruit ripens. Its outside walls dry up and holes appear at the top.

3 Pistil · Stamens

The petals open. You can see the stamens (the male parts of the flower) and the pistil (the female parts).

4 Pollen · Anther

The small sacs at the end of the stamens, called anthers, open. The yellow powder they hold, called pollen, escapes.

5

Bees visit the flower to feed. Pollen grains accidentally rub off on their hairy bodies or on their legs.

8 Pollen

Once fertilization has taken place, the pollen which is left is no longer needed, and it falls off.

9 Petals · Pistil · Stamens

After fertilization, the flower does not need the stamens or the petals any more. They fall off. But the pistil is still needed. It remains strong.

10 Fruit

Inside the pistil, the fertilized ovules are growing to form seeds. They are attached to the inside walls of the ovary. At this stage, the ovary is called the fruit.

The seeds which fall out of the fruit onto the soil in the autumn may grow into new plants the next spring.

12 Wind · Seeds

The seeds break away from the walls inside the fruit. They fall out through the holes near its top when the poppy is blown by the wind.

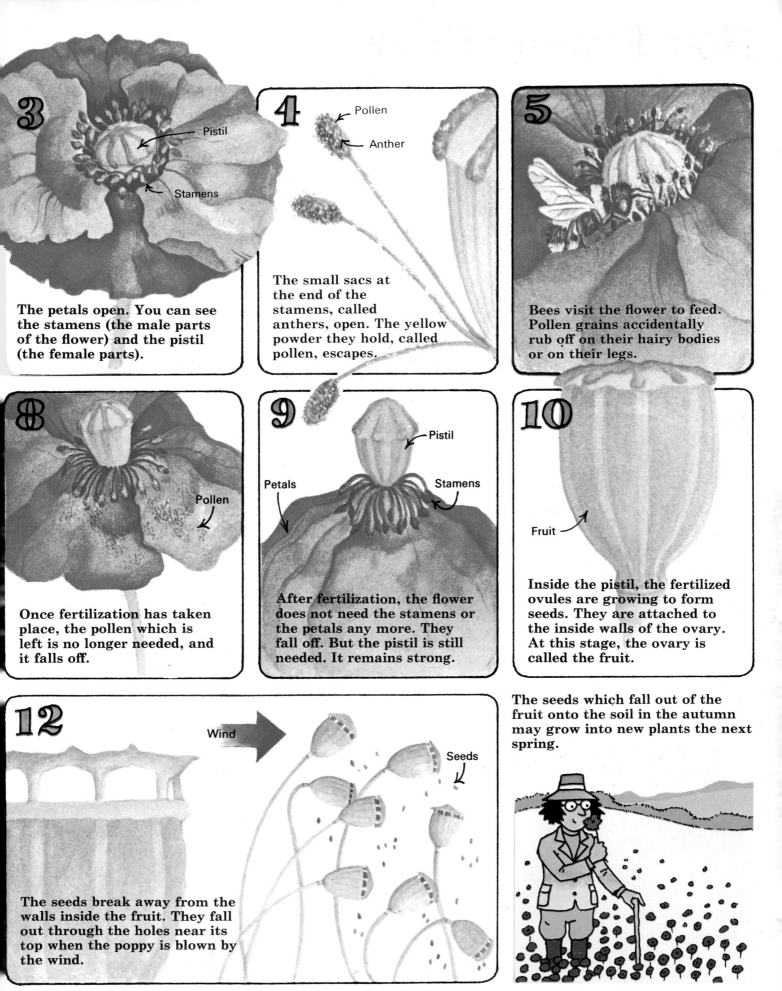

9

How Pollen is Spread

In some plants, pollen from the stamens of one flower can make seeds grow in the ovary of the same flower. This is called self-pollination. In other plants, pollen must go from a flower of one plant to a flower of the same kind on a different plant. This is called cross-pollination. Pollen from a rose cannot make a seed grow in a daisy.

Most plants need insects to carry pollen, but some use the wind. Insects may go to a flower because of its scent or coloured petals. Some flowers have spots or lines on their petals called nectar guides. The insects follow these paths to find nectar.

Sometimes they must brush past the pollen, which sticks to their bodies. When they visit another flower, the pollen rubs off on the stigma.

Sometimes in summer the air is full of pollen, because the wind carries it from wind-pollinated flowers. It can make people sneeze, and give them hay-fever.

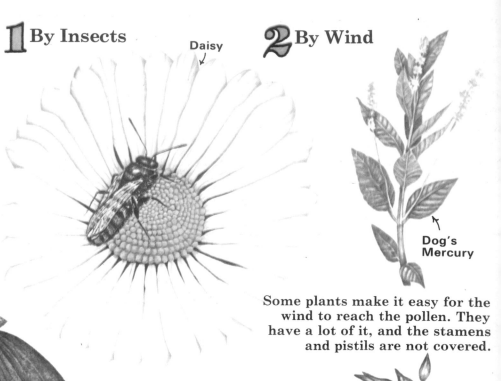

1 By Insects

Daisy

2 By Wind

Dog's Mercury

Some plants make it easy for the wind to reach the pollen. They have a lot of it, and the stamens and pistils are not covered.

Some flowers make the shape of a platform with their petals for insects to land on.

Foxglove

Bees crawl inside some flowers to gather nectar.

3 By Itself

Red Helleborine

Some flowers, like the Red Helleborine, can pollinate themselves.

What Plants Need

Wild flowers need to grow, spread their pollen, and make sure that their seeds are carried away from the parent plant. To do these things, they often depend on the weather, the soil and other living creatures— even people.

PLANTS NEED CERTAIN TEMPERATURES, WHETHER THEY GROW IN COOL OR HOT PLACES. MOST EUROPEAN FLOWERS BLOOM WHEN IT IS WARM

PLANTS NEED A BALANCE OF WATER AND MINERAL SALTS IN THE SOIL TO HELP THEM GROW AND FLOWER

PLANTS NEED LIGHT TO MAKE FOOD FOR THEMSELVES AND TO GROW

SOME PLANTS NEED INSECTS TO CARRY POLLEN

How Seeds are Scattered

Plants cannot produce seeds until they have been pollinated. Then they scatter seeds in different ways. Some use the wind, some use animals, some use water and some scatter their seeds themselves. They produce seeds that will be spread easily in at least one way. New plants need light to grow, so seeds grow best away from their parent plant, which might otherwise shadow them.

By Animals

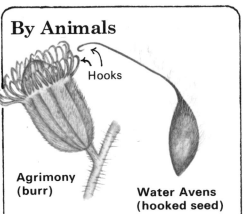

Agrimony (burr)

Hooks

Water Avens (hooked seed)

Some seeds have burrs or hooks that stick to the fur of animals. The seeds drop off the animal away from the parent plant.

By Wind

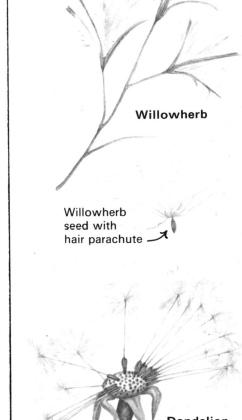

Willowherb

Willowherb seed with hair parachute

Dandelion ("clock")

Some seeds can float on the wind. Dandelion seeds are inside very small fruits, which have hairs that act like parachutes.

By Water

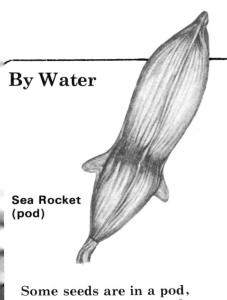

Sea Rocket (pod)

Some seeds are in a pod, like the Sea Rocket pod, that floats in the water until it opens, releasing the seeds.

By Explosion

Fruit

Seed

Policeman's Helmet

Some plants have their seeds in a fruit that pops open. The seeds then shoot out, and travel away from the parent plant. Policeman's Helmet fruits do this.

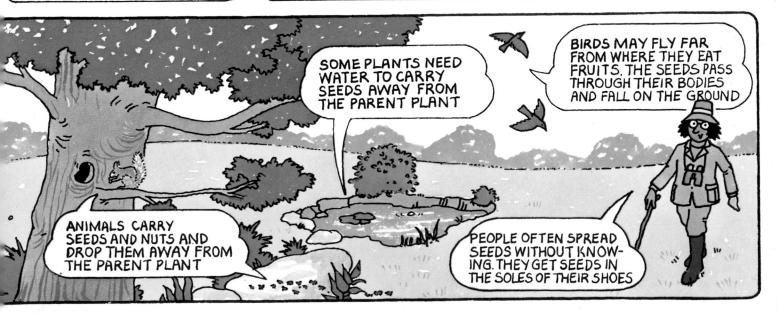

SOME PLANTS NEED WATER TO CARRY SEEDS AWAY FROM THE PARENT PLANT

BIRDS MAY FLY FAR FROM WHERE THEY EAT FRUITS. THE SEEDS PASS THROUGH THEIR BODIES AND FALL ON THE GROUND

ANIMALS CARRY SEEDS AND NUTS AND DROP THEM AWAY FROM THE PARENT PLANT

PEOPLE OFTEN SPREAD SEEDS WITHOUT KNOWING. THEY GET SEEDS IN THE SOLES OF THEIR SHOES

Flower Record Book

Keep a record book of everything you discover about wild flowers. If you use a loose-leaf binder, you can add pages whenever you wish. This is a perfect place to put any maps you have made, or even any photographs you have taken. Remember—anything to do with wild flowers belongs in your record book. Take down the results of your experiments in your book. Draw each step of an experiment as it happens. Write down what you see happening.

A Simple Experiment

Turn a plant away from the light. Come back a few days later. You will see that the plant is leaning towards the light. It is growing towards it because it needs light to make food.

1 Pressing and Mounting

If you pick a common flower you can press it. Put it between two sheets of blotting paper. Rest some heavy books on top.

2

When the flower is completely dry, put a dab of glue on the stem. Stick it carefully to the inside of a clear plastic bag, so you can see both sides.

3

If you find any flower heads on the ground, put them in the plastic bag, too. Stick the bag to a page in your book with sticky tape. Write the name of the flower if you know it and the date and place where you found it.

Common Mallow
Found in a grassy field on July 26th

1 Leaf Printing

Put a leaf onto a flat surface with its underside facing you.

2

Cover it with a piece of thin white paper. Rub back and forth over the paper with a coloured crayon until the shape and veins show through.

3

Stick your leaf prints into your record book.

Common Fleabane
Found in a damp meadow on
August 8th.
at 11am
40cm high
21°C

Collecting Pictures

Stick magazine pictures or postcards of wild flowers into your book. This way you can see wild flowers even in the winter.

WRITE DOWN IN YOUR NOTEBOOK ANYTHING THAT YOU CAN FIND OUT ABOUT CUSTOMS OR FESTIVALS WHERE FLOWERS ARE USED

Drawing and Painting

Make detailed coloured drawings or paintings of the quick sketches you did in your notebook when you were outside. Be sure to write down the time of day when you saw the flowers, since plants may look different in the afternoon from in the morning.

Flower Calendar

You can see different flowers blooming in each season of the year. Make a calendar to help you remember them all. You can also see how a flower changes as the seasons change. Draw it once when it blooms and then draw it again a few months later.

The pictures of the Arum on the right show how different a flower can look at various stages in its life. (Two of the pictures show the inside of the flower.)

Life of the Arum

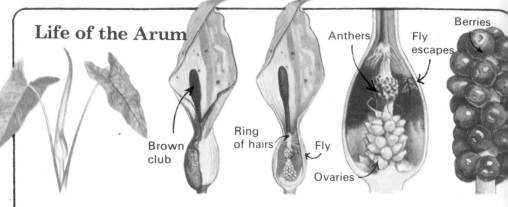

Brown club · Ring of hairs · Fly · Ovaries · Anthers · Fly escapes · Berries

At first, the Arum is green. When the flower opens, it has a brown club. This attracts flies with its smell, and they get trapped inside by a ring of hairs.

They drop pollen on the ovaries. The hairs wither and the flies escape. In autumn, the ovaries develop into very poisonous red berries.

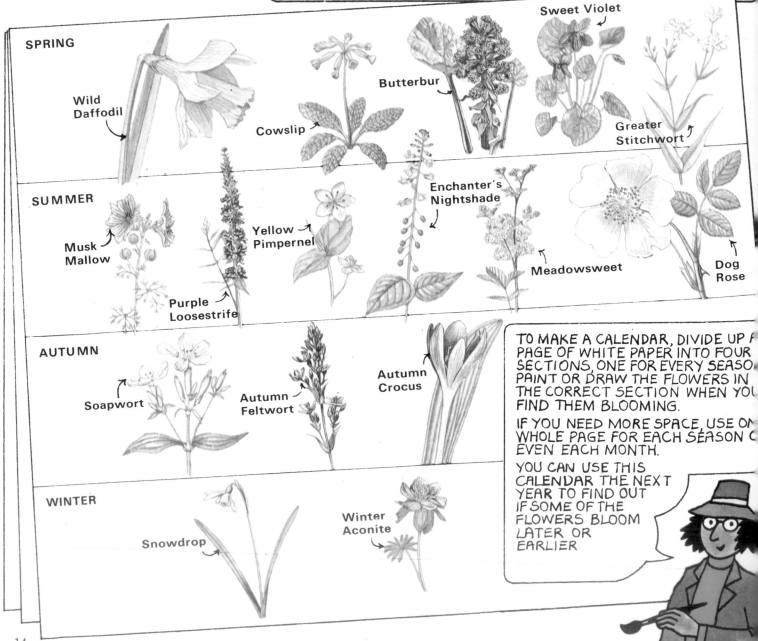

SPRING — Wild Daffodil · Cowslip · Butterbur · Sweet Violet · Greater Stitchwort

SUMMER — Musk Mallow · Purple Loosestrife · Yellow Pimpernel · Enchanter's Nightshade · Meadowsweet · Dog Rose

AUTUMN — Soapwort · Autumn Feltwort · Autumn Crocus

WINTER — Snowdrop · Winter Aconite

TO MAKE A CALENDAR, DIVIDE UP A PAGE OF WHITE PAPER INTO FOUR SECTIONS, ONE FOR EVERY SEASON. PAINT OR DRAW THE FLOWERS IN THE CORRECT SECTION WHEN YOU FIND THEM BLOOMING.

IF YOU NEED MORE SPACE, USE ONE WHOLE PAGE FOR EACH SEASON OR EVEN EACH MONTH.

YOU CAN USE THIS CALENDAR THE NEXT YEAR TO FIND OUT IF SOME OF THE FLOWERS BLOOM LATER OR EARLIER

Rivers and Ponds

Look for plants in different places near fresh water. If they grow in the water, they may be rooted to the bottom or have their roots floating. Their leaves may be under the water or floating on top of it. If plants are growing on the land, they may be at the water's edge, on the banks, or in swamps. Most water plants have their flowers above the surface of the water. They are usually pollinated by insects or wind, not by water.

Yellow Iris

The Yellow Iris has unusual petals and the leaves are very stiff and pointed. Look for stripes on the petals—they are nectar guides.

Frogbit

The Frogbit has shoots that grow sideways. New plants grow upwards from these shoots.

Duckweed

Duckweed can grow to cover a whole pond. It floats on top of still water.

Reedmace

Anthers

Seeds

The seeds of the Reedmace have silky parachutes that the wind carries. You can pick the flower for decoration, as this plant grows in large groups. Let them dry at home and then, if you wish, paint them.

Water Lily

The petals of the Water Lily give shade to pond creatures in hot weather. They can rest on the broad, thick leaves.

Policeman's Helmet

Pod

This flower has its **seeds in a fruit.** When the seeds are fully **grown, the fruit** explodes if anything touches it. You can collect these seeds in the late summer and plant them in the spring.

The Leaves of Water Plants

The leaves of plants growing in the water are of all shapes and sizes. They can be oval, round, short or long. This is because some grow under still water, some grow under fast-moving water and others grow on top of the water.

The Water Crowfoot has broad leaves above the water and thread-like leaves below the water.

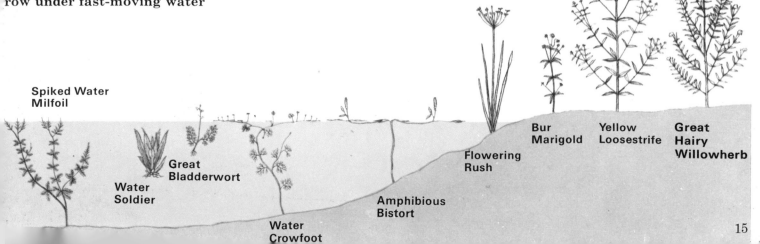

Spiked Water Milfoil

Water Soldier

Great Bladderwort

Water Crowfoot

Amphibious Bistort

Flowering Rush

Bur Marigold

Yellow Loosestrife

Great Hairy Willowherb

Fields, Meadows and Marshes

Fields vary from place to place and so do the flowers that grow in them. Fields can be used for pasturing animals or for growing crops. Meadows are used for growing hay, and marshes are grassy areas which are waterlogged all, or almost all, of the time.

You will find different flowers in different kinds of field, meadow or marsh, depending on what the area is used for, and how wet or dry the soil is. Wet soil is rich in many things that plants need, so you will usually find a lot of flowers.

Marsh Marigold

This flower blooms in wet meadows, and looks like a large, thick-petalled buttercup.

Meadow Clary

This flower is quite common. It can be confused with Wild Clary, which has more jagged leaves and is more rare.

Marsh Thistle
The flowers are in clusters. There are leafy prickles on the dark green stems.

Yellow Rattle
The ripe seeds rattle inside their fruits in the wind.

Common Comfrey
The flowers are bell-shaped and hanging. You can make tea from the leaves.

Red Clover
The flower heads are made up of dozens of sweet-smelling flowers.

Wild Pansy
The flowers are violet or yellow, or a mixture of both colours.

Marsh Orchid

This plant has very unusual pink flowers. You should never pick it, or dig up the roots, as it is quite rare.

The flowers on this page can all be found in damp meadows. You will probably find different kinds of flowers in drier fields, and many of them are illustrated in the charts on pages 28-31. It is important to notice where flowers are growing when you find them.

Marsh Orchids, for example, will often be found in the shade of a tree. Note down as much as you can about the place where you found the flower—what was the soil like in the field? Was there a stream nearby? What was the field used for?

Fruit

Creeping Buttercup
This plant has creeping stems, which root easily.

Meadowsweet
The flowers are in clusters, and smell sweet to attract insects.

Water Avens
The sepals and petals are both red, and the flowers hang in a nodding position. The fruits are easy to spot.

Creeping Jenny
The flowers are bell-shaped and the creeping stems are matted on the ground.

Common Valerian
These red-pink flowers are common near water. They smell very unpleasant. The stem is quite stout.

Water Forget-me-Not
This plant grows near water. It is covered in soft hairs and the flower has a yellow centre.

Hedgerows and Roadsides

A hedgerow is a line of scrub or bushes planted by man, but often other bushes start to grow in between the planted ones. Hedgerows are important because many plants, animals and birds live in them. As fields are mown or ploughed up, living things look for shelter and food there. Many hedges have been destroyed, but people are now trying to save the ones that remain.

Hedges provide shade and shelter for flowers. Look for plants that have grown from seeds trapped in the hedge. They are blown there by the wind.

Flowers growing at the roadside must be tough and strong. They have car exhaust fumes blown at them and litter dumped on them. Only plants that have learned how to spread and grow survive.

Dog Rose
Birds eat the red fruits, called rose hips.

Wild Clematis
The fruits have long white hairs.

Cow Parsley
The flowers form a landing platform for insects.

Honeysuckle
The flowers are pollinated at night by moths.

Greater Burdock
The fruits of this plant stick to the fur of animals.

Stinging Ne
There are stin hairs around edge of the l The flowers green.

Teasel
In winter, teasels are brown and brittle.

Foxglove
These flowers are very poisonous. Do not touch them.

Dandeli
The seed form a feathery "clock", float awa when you blow the

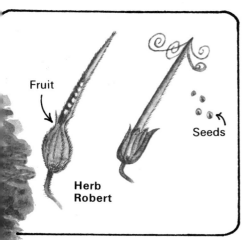

Look for the fruit of the Herb Robert. When the seeds are fully grown, the fruit explodes, and the seeds shoot out.

The Small Tortoiseshell butterfly lays its eggs on the leaves of the Stinging Nettle. If you find any eggs, do not touch them.

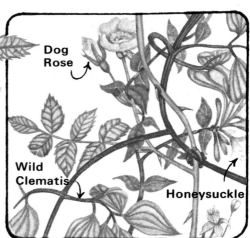

Wild Clematis and Honeysuckle twine themselves round the Dog Rose. It has backward-pointing thorns like hooks, to help it climb.

Make a Scent Jar

Make a scent jar from the petals of any flowers whose smell you like. The Dog Rose, Honeysuckle and Wild Strawberry are good flowers to use. You can put them in a jar or sew little bags from scraps of fabric. Be sure to leave one side of the bag open until you have put the dried petals inside.

Put the petals between two sheets of blotting paper and press them under a pile of books. With a pencil, punch holes in a circle of tin foil to

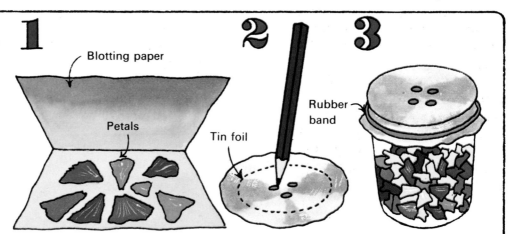

make the lid. When the petals are dry, put them in the jar with some pieces of dried

orange and lemon peel, and a bay leaf. Fix the foil lid over the jar with a rubber band.

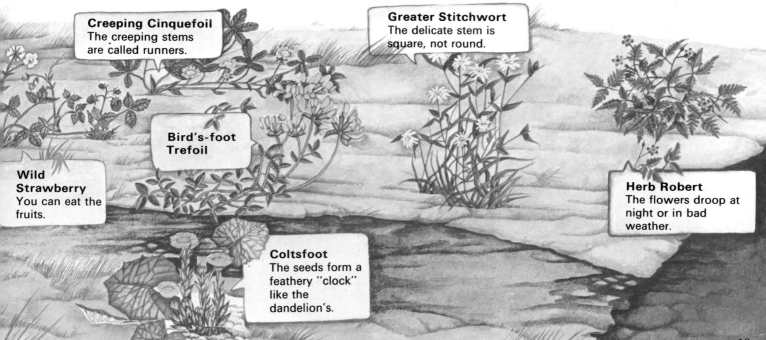

Creeping Cinquefoil
The creeping stems are called runners.

Greater Stitchwort
The delicate stem is square, not round.

Bird's-foot Trefoil

Wild Strawberry
You can eat the fruits.

Herb Robert
The flowers droop at night or in bad weather.

Coltsfoot
The seeds form a feathery "clock" like the dandelion's.

19

Woodlands

When you see big and healthy trees in woods, you may find that there are not many flowers beneath them. The roots of the trees are probably taking almost all the food from the soil and their leaves are blocking the sunlight from reaching the flowers. Some wild flowers that grow in woods bloom in early spring. This is before the leaves on the trees are fully out. The kinds of flowers you will find change with the type of wood you are in and the seasons. Remember to look at the edge of woods. There is enough sunlight there for flowers to grow. See for yourself how many flowers grow near the edge and how many grow where it is very shady. How much of the ground in a wood is covered with flowers?

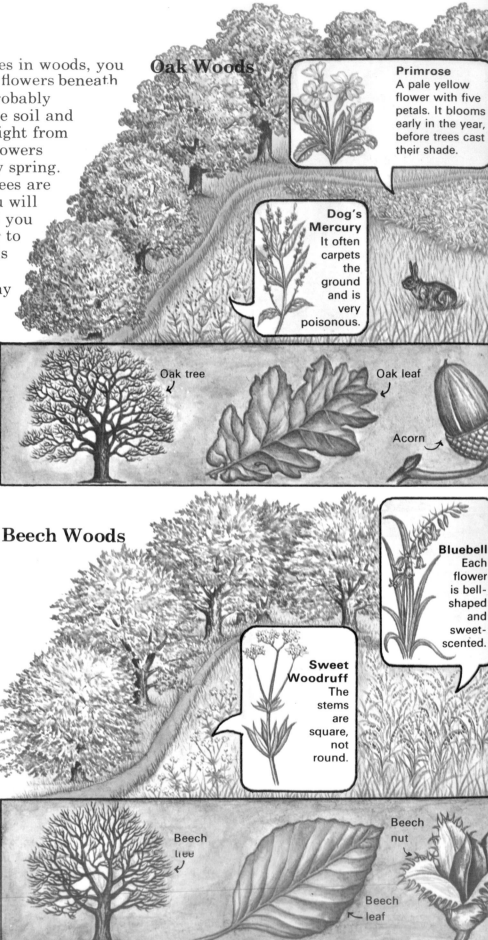

Oak Woods

Primrose
A pale yellow flower with five petals. It blooms early in the year, before trees cast their shade.

Dog's Mercury
It often carpets the ground and is very poisonous.

Oak tree

Oak leaf

Acorn

Beech Woods

Bluebell
Each flower is bell-shaped and sweet-scented.

Sweet Woodruff
The stems are square, not round.

Beech tree

Beech leaf

Beech nut

OAK WOODS
OAK TREES MAY GROW TO BE VERY LARGE. IF THEY DO, VERY LITTLE LIGHT FILTERS DOWN BENEATH THEIR LEAVES. EVEN THE GRASSES NEARBY WOULD NOT GROW VERY HIGH. A GOOD PLACE TO SEARCH FOR FLOWERS IN AN OAK WOOD IS NEAR PATHS AT THE EDGE OF THE WOOD

BEECH WOODS
BEECH TREES GROW BEST WHERE THE SOIL DOES NOT HOLD MUCH WATER. THE FLOWERS YOU WILL FIND IN A BEECH WOOD ALSO PREFER SOIL THAT IS NOT TOO WET. SEE IF THE FLOWERS YOU FIND IN A BEECH WOOD ARE DIFFERENT FROM THOSE IN AN OAK WOOD

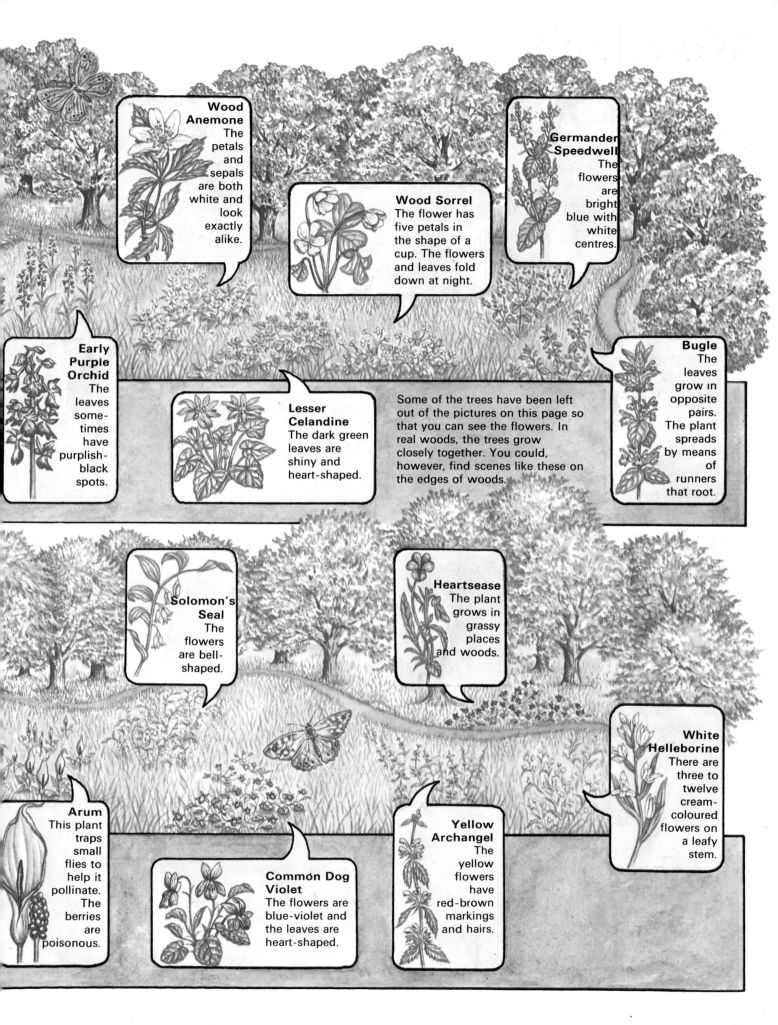

Wood Anemone The petals and sepals are both white and look exactly alike.

Wood Sorrel The flower has five petals in the shape of a cup. The flowers and leaves fold down at night.

Germander Speedwell The flowers are bright blue with white centres.

Early Purple Orchid The leaves sometimes have purplish-black spots.

Lesser Celandine The dark green leaves are shiny and heart-shaped.

Some of the trees have been left out of the pictures on this page so that you can see the flowers. In real woods, the trees grow closely together. You could, however, find scenes like these on the edges of woods.

Bugle The leaves grow in opposite pairs. The plant spreads by means of runners that root.

Solomon's Seal The flowers are bell-shaped.

Heartsease The plant grows in grassy places and woods.

White Helleborine There are three to twelve cream-coloured flowers on a leafy stem.

Arum This plant traps small flies to help it pollinate. The berries are poisonous.

Common Dog Violet The flowers are blue-violet and the leaves are heart-shaped.

Yellow Archangel The yellow flowers have red-brown markings and hairs.

The Seashore

Plants near the sea must learn how to survive. They must find ways to get water and then stop it escaping. To do this, some plants grow a thick outer layer to trap the water, while others have a waxy coat over their leaves, or roll up their leaves when it is very hot and sunny.

Some plants have hairs on their leaves which shield them from the sun and other plants have very small leaves, or grow spines instead of leaves, so that water cannot escape.

Plants must be sturdy enough not to blow over in strong winds. They may have deep roots to grip the mud or stones. The roots also take up water.

Salt Marshes

Salt-Marshes are made of sand and mud. Be careful when you walk there. It is very easy to sink in. Go with a friend and wear rubber boots. The land in such places has slowly taken over from the sea. That is why the soil is salty.

There are different zones in marshes. Different plants grow in each zone. You will probably not find the plants that grow in marshes further inland.

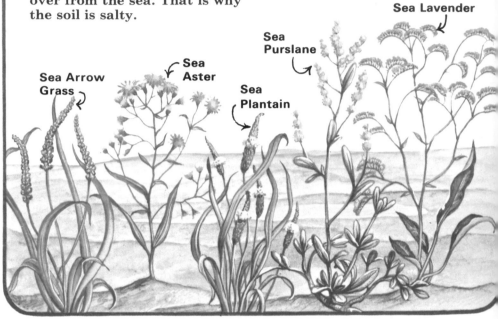

Sand Dunes

There are also different zones of sand dunes. They vary according to how far they are from the sea, and how much they have been built up or "fixed" by the growth of marram grass or other plants.

Shingle Beaches

Not many plants can grow here. These beaches are made of pebbles that once were part of cliffs or rocks. They have been worn down by the pounding of the sea. There is some sand mixed in with the pebbles, but in many places they are constantly shifting. Plants like the Yellow Horned Poppy and the Sea Pea have deep roots that give them some anchorage in the shingle.

Shrubby Seablite

Sea Pea

Sea Bindweed

Yellow Horned Poppy

Cliffs

Plants must struggle to grow here. The wind blows almost all the time and tears up small plants whose roots are not deep. The water drains away quickly, leaving little for the plants and there is almost no soil. The plants must send their roots deep into cracks in the rock.

They sometimes grow along the steep angles of the cliff and are often sprayed with salty water from the sea. Sometimes cliffs have some soil towards the top where you will be able to find land plants.

Be careful when you look at flowers here. Do not climb any cliffs, and keep well back from the edge.

Wallflower

Rock Samphire

Sea Kale

Rock Sea Spurrey

Thrift

Sea Campion

Towns

Flowers grow in waste lands, walls, streets, car parks, gardens, churchyards or any other places in towns where they can find enough soil. Many flowers have learned how to spread in open ground. Some of these flowers are called weeds. Weeds are a problem to people growing other plants, because they take over the land. Many of the seeds of weed plants are spread by the wind, and some by water.

Seed Experiment

Heat some soil in an old pan in the stove to kill any seeds in the soil. Put the pan of soil outside. Do wild flowers start to grow? If so, how do you think they got there?

Ivy-leaved Toadflax
The plant is delicate and trailing, with tiny purple flowers, which have curved spurs. The stems are weak.

Common Toadflax
Each flower has an orange spot on the lower lip and a spur (a horn-shaped tube growing from a petal).

Spur

Rosebay Willowherb
The flowers have four bright pink petals, and the seeds have silky white hairs. It blooms June to September.

Golden Rod
The bright yellow flower heads are made up of dozens of tiny flowers. The seeds have hair parachutes.

Evening Primrose
The flower came originally from America and now grows wild in all parts of Europe.

Wild Chamomile
The plant spreads over wide areas, and has a nice smell when crushed. The petals may point down.

White Campion
This flower is pollinated by moths at night, and the plant has sticky hairs on it.

Oxford Ragwort
The leaves are toothed and the flower heads grow in clusters. The plant grows on bare or waste ground.

Daisy
One of the commonest European flowers. It also grows in short grass in fields. The flowers close up at night.

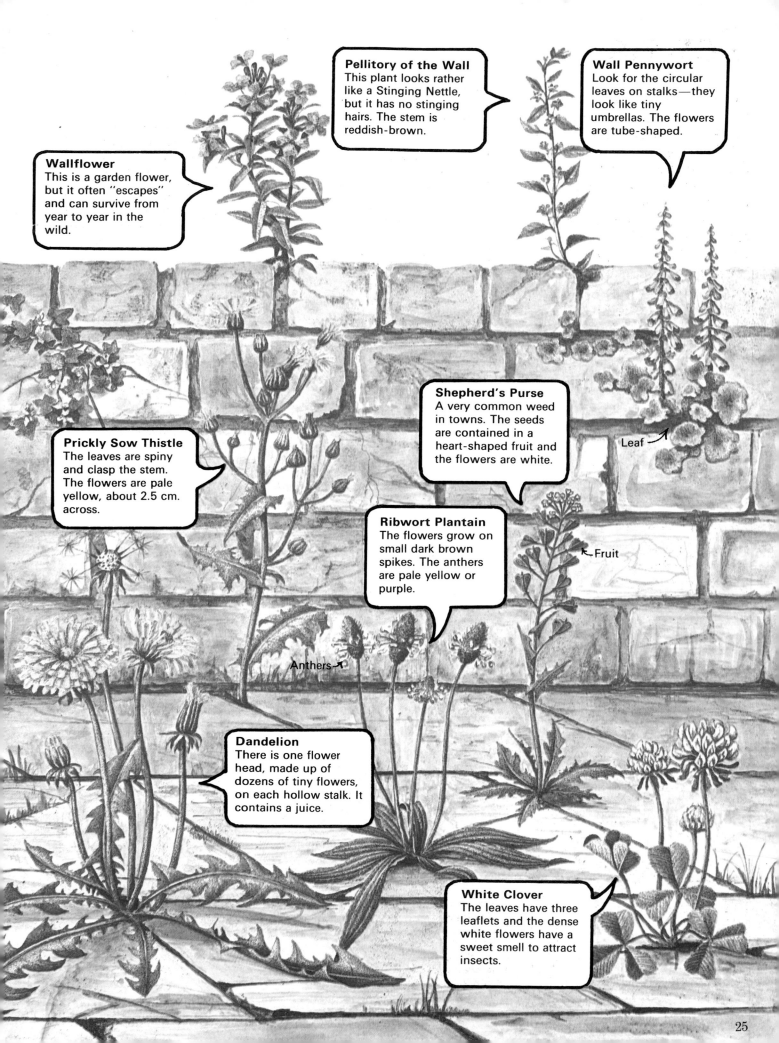

Moors and Mountains

Moors

There are fewer wild flowers that you will find growing on heaths and moors than in fields or meadows. The ones that are able to grow sometimes take over large areas of moorland.

Both heaths and moors are open lands that are swept by wind. Some are very dry and some are waterlogged from time to time. Water collects where the soil is very poor, such as in high land, or areas near the coast.

Different flowers grow on different types of moorland and heath. The most common plant of moorland is heather. It is sometimes burnt to encourage new shoots to grow.

Mountains

The seeds of mountain flowers find it difficult to grow in the poor soils and cold, windy weather of mountain-sides. The higher up a mountain you go, the fewer flowers you will find growing. Trees cannot grow high up on mountains because of the strong winds and lack of soil.

Some plants, however, can grow high up the mountain-side. They are low ones that will not be blown away by high winds. Many flowers that grow on mountains spread by sending out creeping runner shoots which root.

Alpine Bearberry
The plant has white flowers and grows low on the ground. The unripe berries are red, and later turn blue. The blue berries can be eaten.

Bilberry
The plant is shrubby, has blue-black berries that you can eat and red flowers.

Sheep's Bit
The soft blue flowers are in a rounded head and the leaves are narrow. The plant is slightly hairy.

Bog Moss
Areas covered in Bog Moss can be very wet and unsafe to walk on.

Common Heather (Ling)
The plant usually takes over the area in which it grows. Its leaves are in opposite pairs and the flowers are pale purple. The plant also grows on moors and heaths and blooms in August.

Alpine Fleabane
The flowers have yellow centres with pale purple rays around them. The plant is short and hairy.

Common Butterwort
The leaves are broad and their edges roll up to trap and digest insects.

Sundew
The rounded red leaves are covered with long sticky hairs that trap insects and digest them.

Bell Heather
A very common flower on heaths and moors, with needle-like leaves that grow in threes.

Starry Saxifrage
The leaves are fleshy and shiny. The tiny white flowers have pink anthers.

Harebell
The petals of the flower are joined together to form a bell shape. The flowers hang in loose clusters on long, thin stalks.

Opposite-Leaved Golden Saxifrage
The leaves grow in opposite pairs on a square stem. The plant grows low on the ground.

Alpine Lady's Mantle
The leaves have silvery-grey hairs on their undersides.

Moss Campion
The leaves are tiny and pointed, and there are usually many flowers growing together, forming a dense mat on the ground.

Alpine Forget-me-Not
The plant has small blue flowers, and the leaves are soft and downy. The sepals are covered in silvery hairs.

Alpine Milk Vetch
The leaves have four to eight pairs of leaflets, and the flowers are lilac and white, often with purple tips.

Other Common Flowers to Spot

Field Pennycress
30 cm. Waste ground.
Summer.

Sea Rocket
30 cm. Sandy coasts.
Summer.

Fruit (pod)

Fruit

Bladder Campion
45 cm. Waste ground,
grassy places.
Spring/Summer.

Greater Stitchwort
20 cm. Woods, hedges,
fields. Spring.

Star-of-Bethlehem
15 cm. Grassy places.
Early Summer.

Cloudberry
15 cm. Upland bogs,
damp moors.
Summer.

White Stonecrop
Low and creeping.
Rocks, walls.
Summer.

White Bryony
Climbing to 4 m.
Hedges, scrub.
Spring/Summer.

White Dead Nettle
20 cm. Waysides,
waste places.
Spring to Autumn.

Feverfew
30 cm. Walls,
waste places.
Summer.

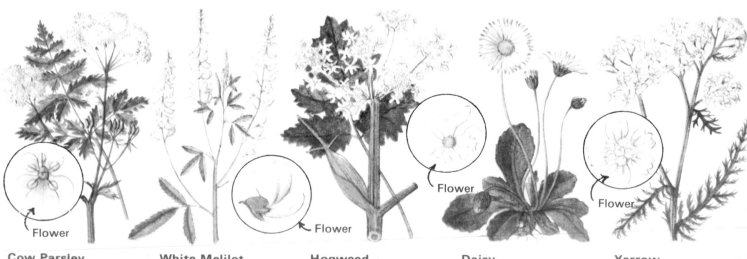

Flower

Flower

Flower

Flower

Flower

Cow Parsley
60 cm. Hedge-banks,
shady places.
Spring.

White Melilot
60 cm. Bare and
waste ground.
Summer.

Hogweed
Up to 3 m. Grassy
places, open woods.
Spring to Autumn.

Daisy
10 cm. Lawns,
short turf, fields.
All year.

Yarrow
30 cm.
Grassy places.
Summer/Autumn.

Remember—if you cannot see a picture of the flower you want to identify here, look on the page earlier in the book which deals with the kind of place where you found it.

The figure given in metres or centimetres is the average height of the flower from ground level to the top of the plant. The season given is when the plant is in flower. The captions also give the kind of place where the flower is most commonly found.

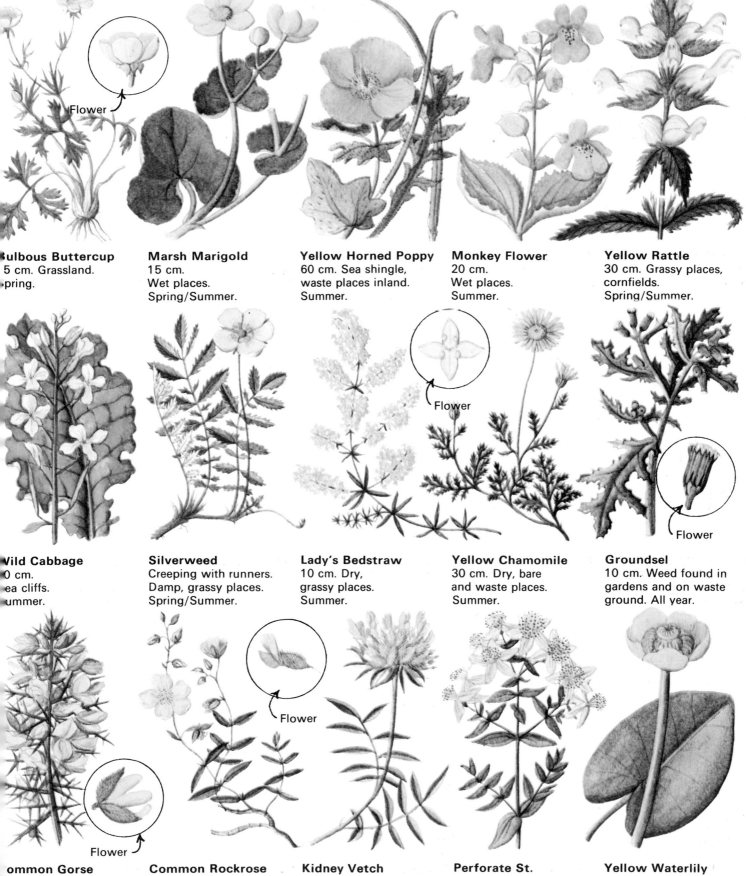

Bulbous Buttercup
5 cm. Grassland.
Spring.

Marsh Marigold
15 cm.
Wet places.
Spring/Summer.

Yellow Horned Poppy
60 cm. Sea shingle,
waste places inland.
Summer.

Monkey Flower
20 cm.
Wet places.
Summer.

Yellow Rattle
30 cm. Grassy places,
cornfields.
Spring/Summer.

Wild Cabbage
0 cm.
Sea cliffs.
Summer.

Silverweed
Creeping with runners.
Damp, grassy places.
Spring/Summer.

Lady's Bedstraw
10 cm. Dry,
grassy places.
Summer.

Yellow Chamomile
30 cm. Dry, bare
and waste places.
Summer.

Groundsel
10 cm. Weed found in
gardens and on waste
ground. All year.

Common Gorse
Grows up to 2½ m.
Heaths, grassland.
All year.

Common Rockrose
Close to the ground.
Grassy and rocky places.
Summer.

Kidney Vetch
15 cm. Dry grassland.
by sea, on mountains.
Spring/Summer.

**Perforate St.
John's Wort**
45 cm. Grassy and
bushy places. Summer.

Yellow Waterlily
A few cms. above water.
Still water, slow streams.
Summer.

Remember—if you cannot see a picture of the flower you want to identify here, look on the page earlier in the book which deals with the kind of place where you found it.

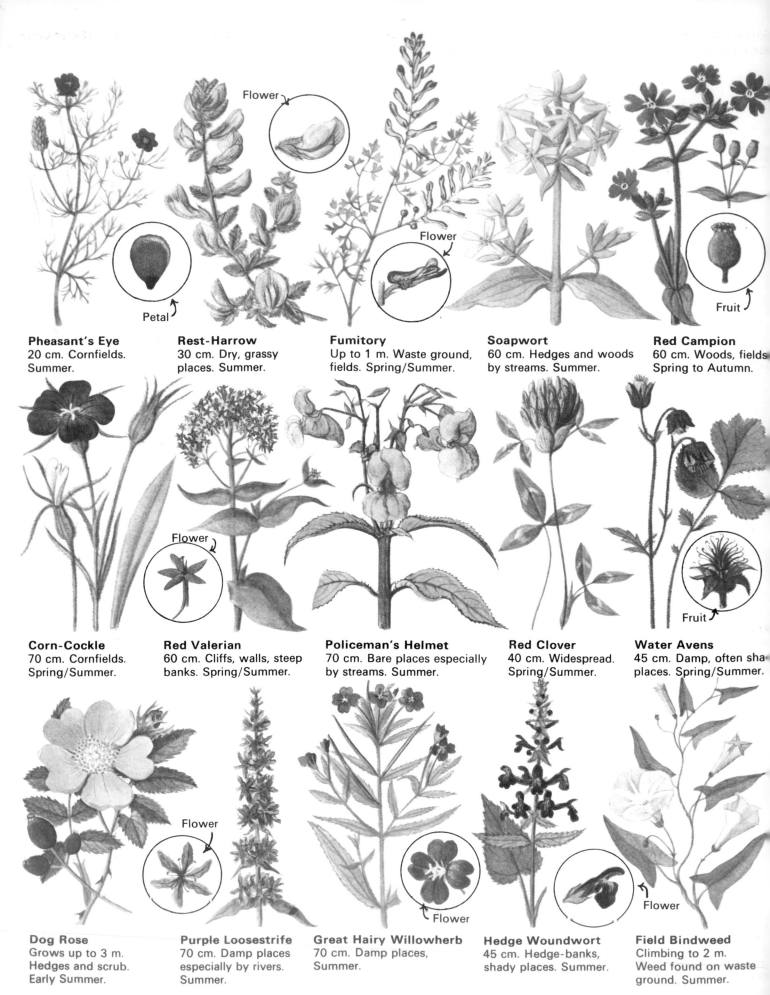

Flower

Petal

Flower

Flower

Fruit

Pheasant's Eye
20 cm. Cornfields.
Summer.

Rest-Harrow
30 cm. Dry, grassy
places. Summer.

Fumitory
Up to 1 m. Waste ground,
fields. Spring/Summer.

Soapwort
60 cm. Hedges and woods
by streams. Summer.

Red Campion
60 cm. Woods, fields
Spring to Autumn.

Flower

Fruit

Corn-Cockle
70 cm. Cornfields.
Spring/Summer.

Red Valerian
60 cm. Cliffs, walls, steep
banks. Spring/Summer.

Policeman's Helmet
70 cm. Bare places especially
by streams. Summer.

Red Clover
40 cm. Widespread.
Spring/Summer.

Water Avens
45 cm. Damp, often sha
places. Spring/Summer.

Flower

Flower

Flower

Dog Rose
Grows up to 3 m.
Hedges and scrub.
Early Summer.

Purple Loosestrife
70 cm. Damp places
especially by rivers.
Summer.

Great Hairy Willowherb
70 cm. Damp places,
Summer.

Hedge Woundwort
45 cm. Hedge-banks,
shady places. Summer.

Field Bindweed
Climbing to 2 m.
Weed found on waste
ground. Summer.

**Remember—if you cannot see a picture of the flower you want to identify here, look on the page earlie
in the book which deals with the kind of place where you found it.**

Some flowers are more widespread in some localities than others—you may be able to find several of one type growing in one area, and none at all in another.

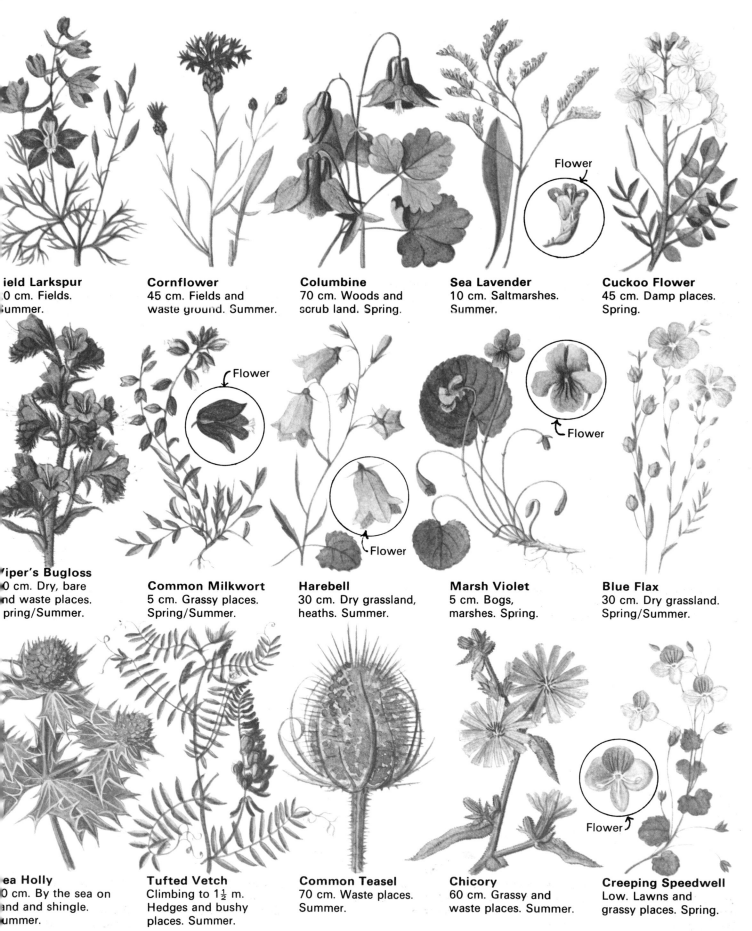

Field Larkspur
0 cm. Fields.
Summer.

Cornflower
45 cm. Fields and
waste ground. Summer.

Columbine
70 cm. Woods and
scrub land. Spring.

Sea Lavender
10 cm. Saltmarshes.
Summer.

Flower

Cuckoo Flower
45 cm. Damp places.
Spring.

Flower

Viper's Bugloss
0 cm. Dry, bare
and waste places.
Spring/Summer.

Common Milkwort
5 cm. Grassy places.
Spring/Summer.

Flower

Harebell
30 cm. Dry grassland,
heaths. Summer.

Flower

Marsh Violet
5 cm. Bogs,
marshes. Spring.

Blue Flax
30 cm. Dry grassland.
Spring/Summer.

Sea Holly
0 cm. By the sea on
nd and shingle.
Summer.

Tufted Vetch
Climbing to 1½ m.
Hedges and bushy
places. Summer.

Common Teasel
70 cm. Waste places.
Summer.

Chicory
60 cm. Grassy and
waste places. Summer.

Flower

Creeping Speedwell
Low. Lawns and
grassy places. Spring.

Remember—if you cannot see a picture of the flower you want to identify here, look on the page earlier in the book which deals with the kind of place where you found it.

Index

Books to Read

The Concise British Flora in Colour.
W. Keble Martin (Ebury/Michael Joseph)
Pocket Encyclopaedia of Wild Flowers in Colour. M. S. Christiansen (Blandford)
The Concise Flowers of Europe.
O. Polunin (Oxford)
Collins Pocket Guide to Wild Flowers.
D. McClintock, R. S. Fitter (Collins)
The Wild Flowers of Britain and N. Europe. R. Fitter, A. Fitter, M. Blamey (Collins)
The Observer's Book of Wild Flowers.
W. J. Stokoe (Warne)
Jarrold Wild Flowers series (6 small paperbacks). E. A. Ellis (Jarrold)

Clubs to Join

The Council for Environmental Conservation (address: Zoological Gardens, Regent's Park, London NW1) will supply the addresses of your local **Natural History Societies.** (Send a stamped self-addressed envelope for the list.) Many of these have specialist sections and almost all have field meetings. **The Royal Society for Nature Conservation** (address: 22 The Green, Nettleham, Lincoln) will give you the address of your local **County Naturalist Trust,** which may have a junior branch. Many of the Trusts have meetings and lectures and offer opportunities for work on nature reserves.

National Organizations

The Botanical Society of the British Isles, c/o Natural History Museum, Cromwell Road, London SW7.
The Countryside Commission, John Dower House, Crescent Place, Cheltenham, Gloucestershire.
The Nature Conservancy Council, 19/20 Belgrave Square, London SW1X 8PY.
The Biological Records Centre at Monks Wood Experimental Station, Abbots Ripton, Huntingdon, co-ordinates survey work of people throughout Britain, to make records of changes in the countryside.